Lorna Cowan has worked in publishing, writing for magazines and websites, for over 24 y[...]
these years, most recently for *Which? Travel*. She moved to Charmouth in 2014 with her hu[...]
past two decades exploring much of west Dorset. Home is now Mintaka on The Street, [...]
carpenter Fred Penny, who was born in Bow House in 1867 and later lived in The Lilacs. F[...]
lived in the house with his family for many years. Mintaka was named by an early tenant, who was a keen [...]
Mintaka means 'the belt' in Arabic, and is a multiple star at the western end of Orion's Belt.
The constellation can be clearly seen from the garden during the winter months.

A row of shops was built on the site of Pryer the stonemason's yard in 1931.

Title Page and Back Cover: Ordnance Survey Six Inch Map of Charmouth in 1904.
Following Page: A view of The Street, looking west.

A Look Back at
CHARMOUTH

Lorna Cowan

CARN PUBLISHING

© Lorna Cowan, 2015.
First Published in Great Britain, 2015.

ISBN - 978 1 9110430 0 3

Published by Carn Publishing,
Lochnoran House,
Auchinleck,
Ayrshire, KA18 3JW.

www.carnpublishing.com

Printed by Bell & Bain Ltd.,
Glasgow, G46 7UQ.

Introduction

The village of Charmouth, just over 23 miles west of Dorchester, the county town of Dorset, sits on Lyme Bay on the Jurassic Coast, England's only natural UNESCO World Heritage Site. This accolade was given in 2001 when 95 miles of East Devon and Dorset coastline were considered to be as important as the Grand Canyon in the USA and Australia's Great Barrier Reef. The coastline is designated for its geological importance, with the cliffs exposing around 185 million years of the earth's history - the Triassic, Jurassic and Cretaceous eras.

The beaches around Charmouth and its neighbouring seaside town of Lyme Regis are world famous for fossil hunting. Ammonites, flat spiral shellfish, and belemnites, squid-like creatures with tentacles, can often be found on the shore. Lucky fossil hunters may also stumble upon larger dinosaurs. The four-metre long scelidosaurus found in Charmouth has never been seen anywhere else in the world. The first ever complete plesiosaur was discovered here in 1824 by Lyme-born fossil expert Mary Anning.

The surrounding countryside is equally as impressive, being part of West Dorset's Area of Outstanding Natural Beauty. Stunning panoramic views can be enjoyed from the many high hills and sea cliffs in the area. A popular hike takes one along some of the South West Coastal Path up to Golden Cap which, at 191 metres, is the highest peak on the south coast.

The history of Charmouth dates from the Iron Age, when a Celtic tribe, the Durotriges, founded a settlement here. The name Charmouth originated from the Saxon word *cerne*, meaning stony river. As the village sits at the mouth of the river, it was known as *Cernmunde*. It appears as such in the Domesday Book of 1086, and records state it had 22 households, three ploughlands and sixteen acres of meadows. There may also have been a small harbour where the River Cerne (now Char) reached the sea as the primary activity at the time concerned the production of salt.

Back then, the Lord of the Manor was Count Robert of Mortain, who was also the half-brother of William the Conqueror, and the greatest landowner in Dorset after the king himself. Soon after, the Manor of Charmouth passed into the hands of a Norman family, the Beauchamps, who later gave it to the abbots of Forde Abbey. Abbot William and the Cistercian monks then founded the 'new town' of Charmouth in the 1290s.

The main road in the village may have existed since Roman days, but it is Charmouth's medieval roots, and the thirteenth century burgage plots that are still well preserved on the north side, that gives the place its uniqueness. Charmouth was designated a Conservation Area in December 1972 and has 33 listed buildings, including The Abbots House which is Grade II*. Around 48 additional buildings all have important and interesting characteristics. The village's historic homes seem to group themselves into three basic types - older sixteenth century to mid-eighteenth century vernacular cottages, Regency and early Victorian villas or large detached houses, and later Victorian houses.

The main building materials used over the years were chert and blue lias limestone, both found locally. Chert is a hard but brittle material, similar to flint, which was mined at the nearby quarries at Hardown Hill, Morcombelake. Much of the blue lias limestone came from Charmouth's beach. Once, many homes had thatched roofing, but as this *Look Back at Charmouth* reveals, these properties were at risk of being damaged or destroyed by fire.

More recently in the 1960s, bungalows and modern homes have been built in the fields along Lower Sea Lane and on the west cliff, with additional housing now behind Devonedge. Charmouth Parish Council state that the resident population of the village is currently around 1,800, though with many properties being second homes and self-catering accommodation, the number of people actually staying in Charmouth will fluctuate during the year. Word is getting out too about how great a place it is - a *Sunday Times* poll in 2014 listed Charmouth as the second most desirable village to live in, losing out on first position to Wellow in Somerset.

The village has also charmed visitors for centuries. Charmouth first developed as a minor resort in the 1850s - the population around that time was just 601 - but it wasn't until the early nineteenth century, when King George III started enjoying holidays in Weymouth, that tourism in Dorset really kicked off. The county's coast and countryside now attract millions of visitors each year. Recent statistics reveal 14.5 million nights were spent in Dorset by visitors, and 26.3 million day trips were made to the area. As a result, 14% of all Dorset employment relates to tourism.

These high numbers translate into good news for the hotels, guesthouses, bed and breakfast establishments and holiday parks in Charmouth. Summer trade in the two pubs, restaurants, shops and businesses is crucial so they can remain open all year round. With the beach huts in Charmouth also now famous thanks to TV's *Broadchurch* (mainly filmed in West Bay, eight miles east along the coast), perhaps visitor numbers will increase more.

Whether a villager or a visitor, you'll sense a great community feel in Charmouth, and there have always been plenty of opportunities to get to know everyone. In the early twentieth century, fetes, complete with a fancy dress parade and band, took place annually. In the years after World War II, locals gathered for the Supper Club, held in St Andrew's Community Hall. Charmouth's firemen would don their aprons and serve food to guests, before entertainment commenced.

Today, neighbours meet up for the Charmouth Traders Association, the Charmouth Local History Society, St Andrew's Church's Changing Spaces project, to run the community library or to attend one of many organised clubs - Knit and Natter, Charmouth Gardeners, the Bridge Club, bowls, badminton, Brownies, to name a few.

There is also a Twinning Association. Charmouth has been officially twinned with Asnelles in north-west France since 1985. The seaside village is of a similar size to Charmouth and relies on tourism for income. It is also in part of France where pro-British feelings run very deep because of the wartime D-Day landings along the coast which involved many soldiers from the Dorset Regiment.

Regular dates for the diary include the Charmouth Challenge, Party in the Park, The George's Beer Festival and the Christmas Day swim. No one needs to worry about forgetting about any of these get-togethers either, as they are all highlighted in the award-winning *Shoreline* magazine. Judges for the People's Project Award were impressed by the work of editor Jane Morrow and her team, and noted the strong community involvement, saying the magazine 'reflected the attitude of the villagers, pulling together to make Charmouth the special and unique place that it is.'

Looking ahead to the future, Charmouth Parish Council are now keen to set up a Neighbourhood Plan, working with the community to prepare a planning policy document, to cover the next fifteen or so years. It will allow local people to have a say, under the Localism Act 2011, over the future development of where they live, what new buildings will look like and where they will be built. As more affordable houses are needed for people born and brought up in the village, it's more important than ever for locals to voice their opinion.

The Queens Armes Hotel

This photograph, dating from around 1965, shows The Queens Armes Hotel, now The Abbots House, in the lower part of The Street. It's one of the oldest buildings in Charmouth, the only Grade II* listed one, and is thought to have been built by Thomas Chard and his fellow abbots of Forde Abbey in the sixteenth century as a resting place for travellers. Over the years, the property has been a private residence following the Dissolution of the Monasteries, an inn, a church manse, then a private home and hotel again.

An inn called The Queens Armes first appeared on the site in the mid-seventeenth century, possibly given the name because it was believed that Katherine of Aragon stayed here in 1501 on her way to marry Henry VII's oldest son, Prince Arthur. Whether she did actually stay, who can say? The County Record Office has no documentation and Katherine's route from Plymouth was not due to pass through the village.

The building does have royal connections though, with Charles II visiting on 22 September 1651. Charles had lost out to Cromwell's New Model Army at the Battle of Worcester and was a wanted man - £1,000 was being offered as a reward for his capture. After hiding at the Sherborne home of Royalist Colonel Wyndham, he was introduced to Captain Ellesdon of Lyme Regis. It was agreed that Charles would set sail to St Malo in France on a boat owned by local seaman Stephen Limbry.

Charles was a distinctively tall man, some eight inches taller than the average man at the time, so he travelled to Charmouth in disguise, along with Juliana Coningsby, a niece of Lady Wyndham. Pretending to be an eloping couple, they booked a room at The Queens Armes and waited for Limbry to turn up. Alas he did not appear - his wife, suspicious he was up to no good, had locked him in the bedroom. Some claim he was locked in the toilet!

Juliana apparently contacted Charles II years later when her son was hijacked by pirates in the Mediterranean Sea and she needed money for a ransom. It is unknown if the king responded.

Today, The Abbots House is a four-bedroom hotel owned by Sheila and Nick Gilbey.

Charmouth's Cement Factory

The building at the far left of this view is recognised today as the Charmouth Heritage Coast Centre. However, long before 94,000 annual visitors turned up to learn about fossil hunting on a UNESCO World Heritage Site, it was the site of a cement factory, having been built in the 1850s.

One of the very early cement works, it used limestone from the nearby cliffs. Boulders found on the east and west beaches were gathered at low tide by horse and cart and taken to the factory for crushing and grinding. The women in the village were paid to gather smaller stones, and they looked forward to south westerly gales when the cliffs took a battering and their baskets were easier to fill.

The business, however, was not profitable and the factory was put up for auction in 1867. In the years that followed, with no buyers, the state of the building declined. That said, locals stored fishing and lobster boats there in the winter. The upper floor became a miniature rifle range and the Scouts used it as their headquarters. Village children thought it was a great place to play hide and seek. It was eventually sold to Charmouth Parish Council in 1938 who used it to store deckchairs and tents.

The Heritage Coast Centre, set up in 1985, encourages safe and sustainable collecting of Jurassic fossils. Around 60 regular volunteers look after the centre and shop today, and assist with family-friendly activities. The nearby blue lias clay cliffs contain many fossils from the early Jurassic period and is the only place in the world where the scelidosaurus, a plant-eating dinosaur about four metres long, has been found. Local fossil collector David Sole discovered the most complete scelidosaurus specimen in December 2000. A life-size cast is on display in the centre.

As with any coastline, the one at Charmouth is forever changing. In 2012 a Pathfinder Research Project, looking at sea-level rises in the future, predicted that the site of the Heritage Coast Centre would be under water by the year 2100.

Thatched Cottages on The Street

Charmouth has had its fair share of famous visitors over the years - Sir Arthur Conan Doyle, Scottish physician and author of the Sherlock Holmes novels, being one of them. In 1894 he stayed at the Coach and Horses Inn while investigating the apparent haunting in an eighteenth-century thatched cottage, one of two pictured here on the left, on the north side of The Street and east of Barr's Lane where the post office, estate agents and Morgans now stand.

Conan Doyle travelled to Charmouth with companions from the Society of Physical Research - a Dr Scott of Norwood, London, and Mr Frank Podmore, a die-hard opponent of spiritualism - and together on the journey south they tried to make sense of the evidence. Conan Doyle stated 'It consisted mainly of a record of senseless noises which made the place hardly habitable for the unfortunate family, who had the house on a lease and could not afford to abandon it.'

The family, described by Conan Doyle as charming, were an elderly mother, a married daughter and grown-up son. The young man stayed awake for two nights with the party and on the second night a fearsome noise broke out, as if someone was whacking a table with a heavy stick. The sound seemed to come from the kitchen but nothing could be seen, and threads stretched across the stairs were unbroken. Conan Doyle continued to sit alone in the dark, hoping the noise would return. But it never did, and he was unable to cast a light upon the mystery.

Any hopes to revisit the property were dashed when the following year the house was burnt down one Sunday afternoon. At that point rumours came into play - was the haunting something to do with the skeleton of a young child that had, years before, been dug up in the garden?

Conan Doyle did not submit a report about the investigation, but Podmore did, blaming the unexplained noises as a hoax, the mischievous doings of the young man living there.

The Lookout

The white lookout tower beside West Beach, still seen today amid pastel-coloured beach huts, was built in 1804 during the Napoleonic Wars, a time when Britain feared a French invasion. Octagonal shaped with a door facing inland and windows on the three seaward sides, the building is one of six similar observation posts in the UK. It was awarded Grade II listed status in 1989.

During the nineteenth century, smuggling along the Dorset coast was rife, so the Lookout was mainly used as a base for the Customs and Excise Service to keep watch over Lyme Bay. The coves and caves located at the bottom of Stonebarrow Hill and Golden Cap, seen here in the distance, provided great hideouts for smugglers and their booty - National Trust trails now allow you to follow in their footsteps.

Around the same time, coastguards working for the Admiralty were responsible for a cannon on the west cliff and ammunition was kept in a hut called the Battery (no longer standing), situated just behind the Lookout. They practised firing the cannon every day, using a target that was fixed in the sea. The 6lb shot was retrieved when the tide was out.

In 1909, the use of the Lookout as an observation post was discontinued, and in 1945 the building was given to Charmouth Parish Council. In recent years, residents of Charmouth are able to enter into a draw to hire it for the summer season. Hiring one of the large beach huts, available from May to September, cost £515 in 2015.

Directly behind the tower you'll find two millstones, weighing approximately one-and-a-quarter tons each, which were used in the cement factory on the foreshore from 1850 to 1867. It is also here you can pick up the Monarch's Way, a 615-mile long footpath that follows the route taken by Charles II in 1651. Starting from Worcester, the path heads to Bristol and Wells, then comes south-west to Charmouth, continues along the Dorset coast over Golden Cap, before turning north up the River Brit to Bridport and Yeovil. After a stretch along the Hampshire Downs and South Downs, the path ends in Shoreham-by-Sea.

The George Hotel

This photo of the George Hotel and the houses to the right of it, situated on the lower section of The Street, was taken in the early 1900s. There is evidence, however, provided by the pub's brewery in 1958, to suggest that a property with that name existed on the site as far back as the seventeenth century - long before the accession of George I in 1714. The Grade II listed building also has a sixteenth century core.

Back in 1703, the George Inn was owned by John Burridge of Lyme Regis, who leased it to a man called James Dober for 1,000 years. Dober paid £60 and the rent of one penny, handed over every year on the Feast of St Michael the Archangel (29 September). By 1760, Walter Oke from Axmouth had bought the pub, along with five other pieces of land nearby, for the sum of £400. John Love was the owner by 1825, and in 1858 the inn was purchased and occupied by J. D. Wheadon, a butcher from Lyme Regis. A family by the name of French were in charge at the beginning of the twentieth century, and today Dean Herbert is landlord.

The room with the distinctive bay window above the front porch was once the waiting room for coach passengers. It was also the best place for smugglers to enjoy a beer as they could easily spot any approaching excise men.

Adjacent to the George is Stow House, a small boarding house at the beginning of the twentieth century, with Bow House next, with its thatched roof and bow windows. Bow House was once a tea room and US troops were billeted here in 1943.

The next pitch-roofed house no longer stands - in its place is Barneys Close, named after Barney Hansford, Charmouth's famous fossil hunter from the 1950s onwards. He had a fossil museum in Firlands House, seen covered in ivy at the end of the row of houses. Firlands House was also a drill hall before becoming the village telephone exchange. During World War II, operator Kate Childs was responsible for telling locals if their loved ones had been wounded or killed. She was nicknamed the 'Angel of Death'.

Charmouth Bridge

The bridge over the River Char at the lower end of The Street was built in 1824 and is one of several bridges in the county that comes with a strict warning. A plaque attached to the parapet states that 'Any person wilfully injuring any part of this county bridge will be guilty of felony and upon conviction liable to be transported for life by the court.'

The stamp of authority comes from a T. Fooks, but little is known about this individual other than he was a man with the power to send criminals on a very long journey. Another plaque, advising persons in charge of 'locomotive traction engines and other ponderous carriages' to be aware of weight restrictions, appears on the bridge over the River Frome at Lower Bockhampton, near Dorchester. This one is signed by E. Archdall Ffooks, alongside his title, Clerk of the County Council of Dorset.

Whether anyone ever 'injured' Charmouth Bridge and ended up on the other side of the world, we don't know. What is certain, however, is that the word 'Dorset', which appeared at the top of the plaque, was cut out in 1940, possibly to hinder any invading German army during World War II. The sign has reverted back to the original wording.

The bridge today, as seen in this 1960s postcard, is a replacement built in 1957 - many local men helped build the walls and parapets. The new bridge is almost double the width of the original one, and a dangerous hump which was narrow and curved, and the cause of several accidents, is long gone. Visibility was also helped during the improvements by lowering the crown by almost three feet, giving drivers a clearer sight line.

A mill house beside the bridge has existed in some form since the 1086 Domesday Book.

The Limes

The Limes, a fine Georgian property named after a row of lime trees in front of the house, was built around the 1820s and is situated on The Street adjacent to Barr's Lane. Now known as Charmouth Lodge, a building has stood on this site since the sixteenth century. In the 1800s a warehouse and workshop were pulled down and two houses erected in their place, later to be made into one large home.

The family of local historian Reginald Pavey lived in The Limes in the 1880s, followed in 1900 by Canon Whittington, his wife and five daughters - Cecil Margaret, Alice Dorothy, Julia Winifred, Ellinor Beryl Maria and Hilda Joan. They were descendants of Richard Whittington, who became Lord Mayor of London in 1937. The family stayed in the house for nearly 70 years. None of the daughters married, but they were involved in church matters, the tennis club, and ran an exclusive school for boys and girls in the adjacent property, now Little Lodge. An advert in 1953 stated that 'all the usual subjects are taught and no pupil is unduly pressed or overstrained.'

The Limes - if all tales are to be believed - could once have been the most haunted building in Charmouth.

Winnie and Joan Whittington told the story of a young sad woman, dressed in white, who would pass them on the stairs. She never disturbed the family, except on one occasion in the 1950s, when a relative, Rev J. Robinson, was playing the piano by candlelight and felt someone grab him by the throat. Another tale is of a monk seen walking through walls and up the path on the west side of the garden, usually on Hallowe'en (the latest sighting was in 1999). Guests also claimed the door of a dressing room would suddenly open during the night. Once a year or so, the sound of hooves could be heard galloping over the roof.

The prominent iron pineapple in the foreground of this photo is on the railings of Littlecote, the house opposite. After being brought back to Europe by Christopher Columbus in the fifteenth century, the pineapple had associations with power and wealth. As a result, architects and craftsmen often sculpted the tropical fruit into gateposts and railings.

Scout Camps

Back in 1907, Robert Baden-Powell held the first Scout camp in history in Dorset, on Brownsea Island near Poole, and Scouts have been coming to the county, and Charmouth, ever since. At the beginning of the twentieth century, Scout tents appeared in almost every postcard of the village showing the area around the beach and River Char, with the fields at the bottom of Lower Sea Lane being one of the most popular places to set up camp.

Instrumental in bringing Scouting camps to Charmouth was local historian Reginald Pavey. Once Head of Clifton Preparatory School in Bristol, he founded 7th Clifton Scout Group in 1909 after a chance meeting with Baden-Powell himself. Pavey was said to be inspired by the first Chief Scout, and from 1920 onwards he encouraged groups to enjoy summer camps in Charmouth, his birthplace.

Scouts - and Guides - came to the village from all over the UK, and this photograph of a happy group, taken in 1925, shows some boys having fun on the beach after an 'all day hike' - the description scribbled on the back of the print.

Although historical records mention the first troop of Scouts was set up in the village in 1914, by a Mr Johnstone and a Mr Simmonds, the 1st Charmouth Scout Group wasn't officially registered until 1965. In the early days, the Scout headquarters were in the old disused cement factory at the seafront. A navy blue flag found there, however, suggests that the group were Sea Scouts - Scout flags are usually green.

Today, fifty years on, the 1st Charmouth Scout Group is going strong, with 23 Scouts, 24 Cubs and 14 Beavers. They are currently extending their headquarters, now in the Playing Fields at the end of Barr's Lane. The 7th Clifton Scout Group donated a generous £300 towards the building fund, in memory of their founder. To mark the occasion of their fiftieth anniversary, the Charmouth Scout Group also erected an eight-foot totem pole, made from driftwood collected from the beach, in the front garden of Charmouth Central, to be enjoyed by all visitors to the library.

Charmouth from Stonebarrow Hill

This view of Charmouth, taken around 1890 from Stonebarrow Hill, clearly shows many of the village landmarks. In the bottom left of the photograph you can see the old school on Lower Sea Lane. The foundation stone for the building was laid by Mrs Breton, the rector's wife, on 25 August 1869 - all the shops closed for the occasion. However, evidence of a blackboard purchased in 1834 suggests a school existed here 35 years before.

A classroom for the new school was built in 1881 and it was further enlarged ten years later. Children had to wait until 1926 for a playground, though.

The school was frequently used for concerts and was the main place for village entertainment before the New Church Hall, also in Lower Sea Road, was built in 1911. The school closed in April 1993 and pupils moved to a new Charmouth Primary further down towards the seafront. The old school was then converted into four private residences.

This view also shows an impressive row of elm trees, standing along the road beside the tennis club. These were cut down in the early 1930s, and a residence, Sandford House, which stood at the corner of Lower Sea Lane and The Street, was demolished in 1958 to allow better access.

In this photograph, at the bottom right, you can see the roof of Charmouth's United Reformed Church, on The Street beside what is today The Abbots House. Rev Benjamin Jeanes was responsible for the building of the chapel in 1815, and died at the age of 55 after 26 years of dedicated service. In those days it was customary practice for church members to be buried under the pew where they had once worshipped. Rev Jeanes asked to be buried in his chapel under the pulpit from where he preached.

Prior to Jeanes, Rev John Brice, a non-conformist minister, sheltered in the seventeenth-century house that occupied this site. He was buried in his chapel in 1716. The last person to be laid to rest inside the church was Fanny Love, buried under her seat in August 1844.

During World War II, the Women's Voluntary Service used the building as a canteen for American troops stationed in Charmouth.

Charmouth House

The old Jacobean building with the thatched roof, on the right of this view, is Charmouth House, situated at the corner of The Street and Higher Sea Lane. Formerly an old coaching house, the property was also known as the Fountain Inn, as well as Charmouth House Hotel, before being converted into private homes in 2005.

Records suggest that part of the building dates back to the seventeenth century. By the early nineteenth century, documents reveal it was a private residence with garden, stables and over three acres of meadow. It was bought in 1873 by George Holly, who turned it into an inn and lodging house, then after his death it became a private residence again, and some years later a boarding house once more.

It's yet another property in the village where some spooky goings-on have apparently taken place. A lady staying in Charmouth House in 1897 was relaxing and looking out to sea in the small sitting room on the second floor in the east wing, when she felt a very vivid presence of a woman beside her. Nothing more happened, but back home in London, when recalling the experience, the lady was shocked to learn that both her mother and grandmother had felt the same presence during their stays in the guesthouse. 'I often wondered why grandmother cut short her visit to Charmouth,' she said at the time, 'but I realise why now.'

Another incident occurred on the night of 29 January 1937, this time in the west wing. A gentleman staying at the hotel woke up in the early hours with a frightful yell, screaming there was a fiendish face at the window trying to tell him something. His wife calmed the man down, saying it was simply a bad dream. But during breakfast next morning, there was a telephone call for him. His mother at the end of the line wanted to let him know his only brother had just passed away.

Caravans at Seadown

Seadown Caravan Park, situated on Bridge Street with direct access to the beach, opened to visitors in the 1960s. The writer of this postcard, sent around that time, commented that there were about 110 caravans on the site. Appearing suitably relaxed on holiday, the sender dated the postcard 'think it's Wednesday!' and described 'wonderful sunshine each day' with 'lots of visitors and cars each day on the beach.'

Today, visitors wanting to stay in Charmouth can park their caravan or pitch their tent at four sites. Starting from the far east of the village, these are Newlands Holiday Park, Manor Farm Holiday Centre, Seadown Holiday Park and Wood Farm Caravan and Camping Park near the roundabout on the A35 towards Axminster. During the summer months, all four can reach maximum occupancy.

A visitor survey, conducted by Charmouth Parish Council in 2010, highlighted that 80% of visitors stay on a campsite or in caravans, and almost 35% of the people who completed the questionnaire were staying in the village for one to two weeks. Some 47% of respondents rated their holiday experience as excellent, with 45% saying they'd definitely be back. Over 61% of people had visited Charmouth before and were keen to return.

Summer in Charmouth also means the open-air market is in town, in a field at the bottom end of The Street, every Monday from the end of May to the end of September. A fun fair operates there throughout August. Both locals and visitors alike enjoy Party in the Park, with live music and fireworks, held twice a year (in May and August in 2015) in the playing fields along Barr's Lane.

In the late nineteenth century, and up until 1914, an event known as the Gooseberry Fair was held every year on 10 July, in The Street opposite the Coach and Horses. Locals recall pink and white striped rock, donkey races and red hot pennies. These were heated in the fire of the bar on a shovel and thrown out of the window for the children to collect.

Fernhill House Hotel

This photograph of Fernhill House Hotel, on the A3052 to Lyme Regis, appeared on auction documents in October 1957, when the property and its twelve-and-a-half acres were auctioned by Rumsey & Rumsey of Bournemouth. Lot 2177 was described as 'ideally placed in unspoiled countryside 450ft above sea level.' Accompanying notes said the property was completely renovated in 1954 and 'various modern improvements [have been] installed to provide the amenities of a good class country hotel.'

The house itself was built in 1837 by Mr R. S. Marker, who bought the land when it was known as Farr's Orchard. Mr and Mrs Marker loved their home and enjoyed a healthy life there, so when the couple died they left it to the Ecclesiastical Commissioners, asking them to form a trust for a local charity. As a result, the house was let out and the rent money used to supply clothing and blankets to the old and infirm poor.

A tenant for five years, Miss Ellen Marryat was the sister of novelist Captain Marryat and a strict Evangelical who set up a Sunday school and bible class in the village. One of her better-known pupils, theosophist and women's rights activist Annie Besant, claimed she was 'a perfect genius for teaching', and asked to be called Auntie as Miss Marryat seemed too cold and stiff.

Annie in her autobiographical writings recalls, 'Daily, when our lessons were over, we had plenty of fun; long walks and rides on a lovely pony; delightful all-day picnics in the lovely country round Charmouth…. Never was a healthier home, physically and mentally, made for young things than in that quiet village.'

Fossil collector James Harrison and his wife were next to live in Fernhill, around 1851. A later tenant, Sir Campbell Munro, built the nursery wing. He was followed by General Eliot, who offered to buy the house for £750. This amount, however, was deemed too low for the charity trustees, but as the time passed and the house fell into great disrepair, it was eventually sold, albeit for a smaller sum.

Current owners, Jo and Rob Illingworth took over the premises in 2006 and the ten-bedroom hotel is now a popular wedding venue with restaurant, bar, swimming pool and crazy golf - the latter on the site of a small boating lake.

Gear's Garage

A road sign currently on the A35 from Axminster highlighting the amenities found in Charmouth includes an image of a petrol pump, suggesting there is a garage in the village. That's not the case these days, but once upon a time there were two, facing each other on the lower section of The Street.

In the late 1930s, one business belonged to George Furnis, who was also captain of the Charmouth fire brigade. The owner of the other garage was William Gear, known to locals as Billy. Born in Charmouth in 1898, he started off his garage business, repairing cars as well as hiring them out, in sheds belonging to Harold Pryer the stonemason. Then, after finding his feet, he moved to the rear of the George Inn. Billy later took over premises next to the Coach and Horses before starting a small garage in Pear Close, near the entrance of Lower Sea Lane. As his business prospered, he moved to a permanent site next to The Queens Armes around 1931, where he was to trade for many years.

This photograph of Gear's Garage, taken in the 1940s, shows employees posing on the forecourt. An advertisement at the time states that the garage stocks Austin, Vauxhall and Standard cars, and you'll be offered 'prompt and efficient repair service' with 'first-class cars and lorries for hire.' The garage even offered excursions to 'places of interest during the season', as well as insurance. Billy flagged up parking too, available in his large car park down at the beach. To call W. A. Gear, in the days when telephone numbers were a lot easier to remember, you simply dialled Charmouth 8.

Billy lived with his wife May in the house named Uphill, situated beside his business on The Street, and from all accounts he worked incredibly hard until his retirement in 1963.

Today, the main garage has been replaced by houses on Queens Walk, built around 2001. The former showroom is now where hungry holidaymakers and villagers queue up to buy their fish and chips at Charmouth Fish Bar and Pizzeria.

Farming in Charmouth

Before tourism took over in the last century or so, farming was the main source of income for those living in much of Dorset. Indeed, over 75% of the county's Area of Outstanding Natural Beauty (AONB) is farmland, but farm types are as varied as the landscape. Cattle and sheep grazing is usual for the steepest or wettest areas, as well as the heathlands, whereas dairy farming is common where the land is more fertile and easily cultivated. Just under a quarter of the AONB is arable, with wheat and barley being the main crops.

This farming photograph is from a personal collection of a descendant of the Norris and Brooks family, who were tenants at Backlands farm and also spent some time at Stonebarrow farm. The entrance to the dairy for Backlands was on The Street, and seeing herds of cows walking down the main road from their fields to the milking barn was not an uncommon sight.

Local farms were where many of the boys and girls in the village would spend their evenings and summer holidays. Flax for rope making was still grown in a number of fields and the children would assist in pulling it. Haymaking was enjoyed by youngsters too, and the money they earned was vital to most working-class families during the early twentieth century.

The straw grown on Dorset farms was also used in thatching. Thatch was the only roofing material available to the bulk of the population living in England's countryside and villages until the late 1800s, so it's no surprise that so many of the properties in Charmouth were thatched. However, this came with a fire risk - not only was water scarce, but until January 1914, the nearest fire brigade was in Lyme Regis.

The new team of firemen in Charmouth were all given a plate to fix to the front door of their homes so people knew who to alert in an emergency. Fire appliances and a hand cart were stored at the workyards of Childs the whitesmith and Pryer the stonemason. Many locals provided ladders. Before the beginning of World War II, a fire station had been built behind The Grange in the lower section of The Street.

Stonebarrow Hill

Stonebarrow Hill, owned today by the National Trust, is a great starting point for 25 miles of scenic walks around the Golden Cap estate. An old radar station, built by the Ministry of Defence in the 1950s, is now used by the Trust as a shop.

Stonebarrow reaches an elevation of about 155 metres, and although not quite so steep as its neighbouring Golden Cap at 191 metres, for Miss Sheila Angus who lived in Bow House on The Street, it was the perfect place to indulge in her winter hobby - skiing!

For the past 30 years, though, it has been runners who have raced down the section of hill in this view, past the ruins of a farm barn, in the final stages of the Charmouth Challenge. Organised by Charmouth's Primary School Parents, Teachers and Friends Association to raise funds for learning opportunities, the Charmouth Challenge takes place every year in June or July and is recognised as the most southerly fell race in England. The eight-mile course goes through some of the finest coastal scenery in the south west, and includes an ascent of Golden Cap.

Back in 1886, another race took place in the village and was entered by twelve-year-old Charles Burgess Fry - later to represent England in both cricket and football. He was staying in a guesthouse and wrote a letter some years later describing the event:

'The athletic sports in which I won my first race ever were part of the regatta,' Fry recalled. 'The race was a steeplechase. The course, which was vague, started on the grassy incline on the right bank of the lower Char near the beach, went across some fields in the dip and finished on the grass slope where it started.' Just over half a mile, the race ended in a sheer sprint. 'I won easily and Kirby [the son of a doctor] - the only other competitor in proper running vest and knickers - was second. It was then I discovered I could run!' Fry's prize was 10 shillings, which he had to collect from the chemist.

St Andrew's Community Hall

This photo of St Andrew's Community Hall, an Arts and Crafts-inspired building, was taken before restoration work commenced in 2010, and shows the building with its old front porch which has now been replaced by a two-storey extension matching the height of the hall. Funding for this project, a substantial £50,000, came from the Big Lottery Fund. More money, this time £9,000, has recently been received from the Dorset Community Foundation. Energy efficiency improvements are now being planned for the main hall.

Charmouth Church Hall, as the building was previously known, came about as the result of some remarkable fundraising by villagers. The sum of £650 was needed to build a hall - on land donated by Douglas Pass, the Lord of the Manor - and it was a wonderful day on 3 December 1910 when everyone's efforts were celebrated and Mrs Whittington of The Limes set a commemorative stone into the wall as building work started.

Fundraising activities had included a summer market, held in August 1908. Shooting competitions also took place. A list of donations was put together showing, in descending order, who had contributed what. A Charmouth Birthday Book 1909 was published too. Hard-backed and pocket sized, no record exists revealing who was responsible for compiling the book or indeed the cost, but it would have been a time-consuming project. Beside every date there is the name of the person making the donation, who had presumably chosen their own birthday or that of a loved one, as well as a small verse. There is also space to add personal notes.

Just over fifteen months after the foundation stone was laid, Charmouth Church Hall opened on Easter Tuesday 1911. The village band led a procession through the streets and around 300 people turned up to cheer.

In the years since, the hall has been used for a variety of events, including the fondly-remembered Supper Clubs, first held to welcome home those who fought in World War II. Women brought along their crockery from home and local firemen became 'waitresses' for the evening. Concerts have taken place - Glenn Miller allegedly played to American troops during the war - and pantomimes have been performed. Today, the hall is also used by the Badminton Club and Brownies.

The Footbridge over the River Char

The River Char runs a few miles from Bettiscombe in Marshwood Vale through Pilsdon and Whitchurch Canonicorum before turning down to Charmouth. According to the Environment Agency, the typical river level range near the footbridge that takes you over to East Beach is somewhere between 0.05 and 1.13 metres, but as locals and frequent visitors know only too well, the river has a mind of its own, and not only does it often change its course, during the storms of February 2012 the water rose to a record level of 3.76 metres.

This postcard view, taken around the 1950s, shows the footbridge that was officially opened in August 1930 by Mrs West, who lived in Luttrall House on The Street. Her husband, John, was a engineering contractor from Rochester, Kent, and when the River Char altered its course in 1906 and the existing bridge was washed away, he set about building a replacement, along with Charmouth-born carpenter Fred Penny and other local craftsmen. The Parish Council had asked for tenders for a new bridge and one Bristol firm estimated it would cost £310. West was able to construct his for just over £193.

The footbridge that we cross today was opened in April 2011, and replaced West's bridge which was in a deteriorating condition and inadequate for the number of pedestrians using the crossing - around that time a council report highlighted that the bridge was crossed more than 700,000 times a year, and the number of people making the crossing went from nearly 16,000 in January to 168,000 during the peak holiday time in August.

The current bridge, approximately 80 metres upstream from the beach, measures 30 metres long and has a clear width between the handrails of one metre. It allows for some resting space, a stopping place to feed the ducks and swans, and a viewing point to look at the unique landscape on a World Heritage Site. A year after its opening, the bridge received an award from the Institute of Civil Engineers and was praised for its 'practical and interesting design, which arose from a real engagement with the people who would be using it and sensitivity to the setting.'

Top of The Street

This old postcard view of The Street, just west of the entrance to Higher Sea Lane, shows the upper part of the village which was once full of shops and businesses.

Claremont, the Victorian building on the left-hand side with the bay windows, was occupied by a fortune teller during the mid-1800s. Her predictions, however, came true so often that eventually she refused to tell people what she saw. The property was later a boarding house, run by Alfred Hodges, and remained as that until 1962 when the house was turned into flats.

Across the road, the shop with the sheet over the window (Granville House today) belonged to a bootmaker Fred Hutchings, who purchased it in the early twentieth century. It was inherited by his sons Ernest and Fred. Almost 100 years before, in 1814, another shoemaker or cordwainer, John Potter, lived here, followed by his son William. One Christmas Eve in the 1880s, he watched his home burn down while sitting on a chair placed on the street opposite. Fortunately, an insurance company rebuilt it, and the next tenant was W. G. Copp, a tailor.

Waterloo House, next up on the right, was bought in 1803 by Benjamin Diment, a Whitchurch Canonicorum yeoman. His son, Benjamin the Younger, turned it into a blacksmiths - he made the iron railings for St Andrew's Church in 1836. The house has been altered over the years; sometimes being three homes, at other times two. It was bought in the late 1880s by H. P. Childs and left to his son A. B. Childs, who was a whitesmith and water bailiff. In the 1990s the entrance to the forge was through an archway. Today this leads the way to the only shop now left at this end of Charmouth, Old Forge Fossils.

The three-storey house with the three dormer windows is now known as Melville House, but a grocery business and post office opened here in 1937, run by Nora and Ellis Long. Ellis was also a talented artist and in his studio at the top of his home he painted colourful posters for the Regent Cinema in neighbouring Lyme Regis.

Charmouth Lawn Tennis Club

The Lawn Tennis Club in Charmouth, located on the north side of Lower Sea Road, was founded in the early 1880s and is reported to be the oldest club in Dorset. The site was originally garden allotments, and then it became a croquet club with two lawns, leased by the Pass family who were large landowners of neighbouring Wootton Fitzpaine. The lease stated that if the club still existed in 75 years' time, then it would have the right to own the land, and that's exactly what happened in 1968.

The tennis club, like many others in those days, was extremely elitist and only high-ranking service officers, doctors, lawyers, landed gentry and those of independent means were allowed to join. While General Eliot and George Pavey seem to have been the original founders (with James Scalch of The Court as secretary), it was four of its members - Beryl, Winnie, Dorothy and Joan Whittington who lived at The Limes - who played an active role in running the club from the early part of the twentieth century. The youngest sister Joan is seen in this photograph, taken in 1950 with her Mixed Doubles Final partner, a Mr Evans. She was a skilled tennis player and had at one time been accepted to play at Wimbledon. However, it was discovered that Joan had already taken part in a competition in Cairo, and as she had won prize money she was not allowed to compete.

The Whittingtons also helped to organise a tennis tournament, held each year in Charmouth during the month of August. Many well-to-do families spent their holidays in the village, simply so they could attend and play. Competition could be tough. Maud Watson, the first female Wimbledon champion, joined the club in 1916 (and lived in Charmouth until her death in 1946). W. J. Turnbill, another Wimbledon player, visited in 1923. Other well-known club members included novelist Ernest Temple Thurston and Lady Orpen, wife of the famous artist. Tournament prizes were usually Boots the Chemist vouchers, and a grand ball would take place when all matches were over.

Today, the private club, accredited to the Lawn Tennis Association, has four courts, one being an all-weather tarmacadam court.

St Andrew's Church

The Parish Church of St Andrew, situated halfway up The Street on the left-hand side, is a Grade II listed building made of local stone, some quarried from Hardown Hill near Morcombelake. The church was built in 1836-38 in a Gothic Revival style by architect Charles Fowler (who also designed London's Covent Garden Market) and replaced the Church of St Matthew which had previously stood on this site since the early sixteenth century.

In 1835, it was announced to the congregation that St Matthew's Church was unsafe and it was necessary to knock it down and start again. Concerned, the whole village set about raising money and donations came in from locals, friends outside the parish and even schoolchildren.

Today, the community is once again focused on a restoration project - Changing Spaces - at St Andrew's Church. With repairs needed to roofing, stonework and woodwork, as well as a general refurbishment, it is hoped financial aid will come from the Heritage Lottery Fund in 2016. There are ambitious aims for the future, for the church not only to be a place of worship, but also a building that can host concerts, exhibitions and art performances.

In St Andrew's old graveyard, near the main entrance to the church, you'll find the large tomb of Lieutenant James Warden, who died in a duel at Hunter's Lodge on 28 April 1792. Lord of the Manor Warden was known to be argumentative, and would often fall out with locals. He took legal action in 1789 against the vicar at the time, Rev Combe, and against others for removing sand and seaweed from the beach. However, after being abusive towards neighbour Norman Bond, and threatening to shoot his dogs, Bond challenged him to a duel. Warden took the first shot, but it went straight through his opponent's hat. Bond, being a better marksman, then aimed at Warden and shot him through his heart. He died instantly.

Interestingly, Warden's wife made no effort to prevent the duel, and even chose the pistols. Indeed, it would appear that she was keen to be rid of her husband, as if he didn't lose the duel, she made it clear she wanted him hanged.

East Beach

We may not see cows today on Charmouth's East Beach, but the stretch of coast heading towards Seatown is popular with fossil hunters, sun worshippers, swimmers, surfers and fisherman. One such fisherman, Isaac Hunter, was born in the village in 1833, and is well remembered for his heroism. The descendant of a Scottish laird, Isaac was a powerful oarsman, and although he would often challenge others to a race between West Bay and Lyme Regis, no one ever took him on. It is said that on one occasion Isaac rowed all the way from Charmouth to Plymouth, and he made claims that he'd even ended up one time in Cowes on the Isle of Wight.

It is Isaac's famous dream, however, that locals often recall. On 24 November 1872, during a bad storm, Isaac dreamt that someone was interfering with his lobster pots, which were on a reef below Westhay farm near Golden Cap, seen in the distance in this old view. The dream was so vivid that he told his wife he was off to investigate, but hearing the rain batter down outside, Mrs Hunter ordered him to climb back into bed.

The dream kept recurring though, so eventually Isaac got up and, despite the wind and rain, made his way to the beach with his son. A coastguard warned about the dangers of walking along the sand, but Isaac was determined. As the men turned round part of the cliff where their lobster pots were located, they saw a ship being beaten by the waves. It was dark, and it was difficult to see what was happening, but Isaac realised those aboard were in distress. He rushed to wake the farmer at Westhay, and after clambering back down the cliffs, he managed to rescue three of the four crew of the French boat. The survivors, well aware of their fate if Isaac hadn't come to the rescue, later presented him with a silver watch, inscribed with a message of thanks.

View from Cain's Folly to Lyme Regis

Cain's Folly is the name given to part of the cliff face on Stonebarrow Hill which was once covered in beech trees but is now crumbling into the sea below. Concrete buildings situated here, used by the RAF for coastal radar coverage during World War II, slipped over the edge on 14 May 1942.

This postcard, taken from Cain's Folly around the 1930s, looks west towards Lyme Regis, just over two-and-a-half miles away. Much of the land on the coast is owned by the National Trust, with the Black Ven area, and the Spittles behind, being acquired between 1966 and 1968. The Black Ven is the most extensive coastal mudslide area in Europe, and although you can walk along Charmouth's West Beach when the tide is out, much care needs to be taken.

The pretty seaside town of Lyme Regis is famous for its fourteenth-century curved harbour wall, the Cobb, which featured in the 1981 film *The French Lieutenant's Woman* starring Meryl Streep. Stone steps, referred to as 'Granny's Teeth', are also mentioned in Jane Austen's *Persuasion*.

A famous resident of Lyme Regis was Mary Anning, born in 1799. After her father, a cabinet maker, died when she was 11, Mary would search for fossils to sell under the blue lias cliffs. It was dangerous work and in 1833 a landslide, which narrowly missed her, killed her dog Tray. However she continued to become one of Britain's most influential fossil collectors - her discoveries included the first ichthyosaur skeleton correctly identified, and the first two plesiosaur skeletons.

Although well-known around the world, Mary, as a woman, was not eligible to join the Geological Society of London. It was only 163 years after her death that she was included in the top ten list of women who have most influenced the history of science.

This view of Lyme Regis is also one that caught the imagination of Joseph William Turner, one of the greatest masters of British watercolour landscape painting. Sketches of *Lyme Regis from Charmouth Beach*, done in graphite on paper in 1811, are part of the Tate Gallery collection. There is also a small oil painting entitled *Shrimpers at Lyme Regis*, on display at Nunnington Hall in North Yorkshire, which has recently been attributed to Turner.

The Royal Oak and Little Hurst

This photo, taken in 1890, shows two boys standing beside a horse and cart on The Street. To their left is the Royal Oak pub and Little Hurst. To their right, the gated entrance to The Court.

A pub first appeared on this spot around 1867, when the licence of an inn on Lower Sea Lane was transferred to a butcher's shop here, and the home of village crier John Wild. Every time a boat with coal arrived in Lyme Bay, Wild yelled loudly and earned himself a shilling. Prior to that, in 1814, the property appears to be owned by Catherine and Fanny Love who were linen drapers and tea dealers.

Palmers Brewery of Bridport purchased the premises in 1896, when the tenant was Catherine Barnes. One of the better known landlords though was Jim Bridle, who took over the reins in 1923. Lyme-born Jim had been in the Royal Navy for 25 years. He was on the ship with Marconi in 1901 when the radio pioneer made his first successful long-distance wireless call. He met Captain Scott in South Africa, en route to the Antarctic on *Discovery*. Bridle also rubbed shoulders with royalty when he was an attendant at the Albert Memorial Chapel at Windsor Castle. Here he spoke to the Archduke of Austria, a few weeks before he was assassinated. Bridle retired as landlord in 1934 and moved to a house in Higher Sea Lane. He named it after the first foreign soil he had landed on - St Helena.

Today, The Royal Oak is run by Karen Phillips and Ian Hendry. It's a popular Dorset pub name, referring to a tree in Boscobel, Shropshire, where Charles II hid from Cromwell's army. The king also hid in Lee Lane, Bridport, where there is a memorial stone.

The house next door, now Charmouth surgery, was owned by Lord Herbert, who set up a convalescent home with twenty beds in 1857. Florence Nightingale attended the opening ceremony. Towards the end of the 1880s, the property was bought by J. H. Harrison, a partner of Harrison and Sons, Printers in Ordinary to Queen Victoria. Harrison had lived in The Hurst, Regent's Park, London, hence the name Little Hurst.

Newlands School

Situated at the bottom of Stonebarrow Lane, on the bend of the road coming in east from Bridport, is a large self-catering property offering accommodation for up to 38 people. Stonebarrow Manor, as it's been known since 2002, is popular for family gatherings, group reunions and corporate training breaks. Back in the early 1900s, however, the building was home to Newlands School.

Although not seen clearly in this photograph, taken around 1922, a large orchard occupied much of the front garden. The fruit from the trees was stored in a barn left of the main school, now renovated into a modern home. A walled garden can be found at the back.

Owner Tom Murphy says guests often visit in the hope of seeing a ghost, but he himself has not met any. That said, he does recall a night when he heard girls' screams coming from the garden, but a quick dart outside revealed no one to be there.

Newlands School hasn't been the only teaching establishment in the village over the years. Local children and those from surrounding areas were taught in the school at Lower Sea Lane, and an exclusive school was run by the Whittington sisters at Little Lodge. There has also been another, on Axminster Road. A Mrs Aplin came to Charmouth from the Bristol area in 1883 and ran a school for many years in Thatched Cottage. The local School Board complained that Mrs Aplin's school interfered with the attendance at the Board School. However, a letter in the log book states that should the school at the top of the village close, the class of children who attended were not likely to move to the Board School.

The log book also shows that attendance at the Board School was often poor, and not because pupils were studying elsewhere. Entries state that the number of children attending school was low due to, 'several off catching mackerel', 'many gathering acorns and apples', and some boys missing on 5 November as they're 'parading their Guy around the village'.

Devonedge

The impressive three-storey building, seen in this early twentieth century view, is known today as Devonedge. Travel back a few decades though, and here you would find a little baker's shop with a thatched roof, owned by Frank Coles. A bake-house, sheds and orchard extended behind the property as far back as Charmouth Meadows (the Playing Fields). In 1891, Frank married Lillian Dare of Wootton Fitzpaine, and she looked after the shop with her sister Bessie. Frank delivered bread in his cart.

Sadly, though, like many thatched properties in the village, the shop caught fire in 1894 and was destroyed. But not perturbed, the Coles simply decided to build another, somewhat more elaborate, building to take its place. The end result was Sunnyside, a large lodging house.

Coles employed local masons Gollop and Hahn to do the building work, but it wasn't the most straightforward of projects. The west wall adjoined a property belonging to Harold Pryer, another builder, who was not on speaking terms with his neighbour Coles, so he refused to allow scaffolding on his land. As a result, workmen were forced to do without and had to lean over and plaster each row of bricks from the inside.

Sunnyside guesthouse has several sets of rooms and initially it was popular with visitors. However, it didn't really pay. The property was to become the village post office, then in the middle of the twentieth century, a Mr Harris of Lyme Regis bought the premises and turned it into flats.

The hedge visible on the left-hand side of The Street surrounded Pryer's workshop and building yard. A carved figurehead of a life-sized lady, that had been washed up on Charmouth beach, used to stand in the grounds. The land belonging to Pryers & Sons was sold around 1931 and four shops were built. The first was a lock-up shop which then became a gift shop. A hairdressing business opened, followed by a chemist. Lloyds Bank later appeared. Pryer's workshop with its distinctive cross on the roof was purchased by J. R. W. Bragg of Lyme Regis and converted into a grocer's shop. Reggie and Elsie Bragg ran the business until the late 1950s, when it was taken over by Andrew and Anne Peach. It is the chemist today.

Lower Sea Lane and Higher Sea Lane

This postcard of Charmouth, taken from the cliffs around the mid-twentieth century, clearly shows the changes that have occurred with regards housing during the last 50 years, especially around Westcliff Road, Five Acres and Double Common. Even just a century or so ago, the 1903 Ordnance Survey map shows only a few buildings along Lower Sea Lane - the school, almhouses, coastguard cottages, Green Gates and Sea View. Previously called Sea Side Lane, it was just that - a narrow hedge-bordered lane taking you down to the sea.

Sea View, seen on Lower Sea Road in the bottom right of this view, was a house built on a piece of ground referred to by locals as 'the potato plot'. It was purchased in 1837 by Rev J. D. Hales and rented to Robert Hunter, who had ten children - five sons and five daughters. Robert appears to be a man of all trades, for he was a fisherman, a pleasure boat owner, a bathing machine proprietor, and a well-known smuggler. When he died around 1883, his funeral procession to the chapel was the longest the village had ever seen. The family are also remembered for having a stuffed shark hanging in their shed.

The large house, diagonally opposite to the left, seen on what is Hammonds Mead today, is Hammond Mead's Hotel, which was demolished in the 1980s as building work for the new primary school commenced.

All the houses on Higher Sea Lane, formerly called Rockett's Lane, have been built since the beginning of the 1900s - all except the towering Sea House, which appeared in the late 1700s. It went on to become Gresham House before being opened as a boarding house - Sea Horse Hotel - towards the end of the nineteenth century.

Higher Sea Lane came to an end at Double Common, where there was a gate leading into Higher Sea Fields and a path to the beach, land belonging to the Lord of the Manor. It was rented to William Morris of Backlands farm. Thalatta, the house to the far left, was built in 1922.

Coach and Horses Hotel

The Coach and Horses Hotel, seen on the right of this 1950s postcard, offered overnight accommodation in eight bedrooms, as well as a residents' lounge and two bars. The brick three-storey property was built in the early 1900s to replace a thatched two-storey coaching inn originally on this site, which had been destroyed in a fire in 1882.

The inn was of great importance during the coaching days of the 1840s when seven or eight stagecoaches would pass daily through the village. The 'Exeter Flyer' travelled from Exeter to London, going through Honiton, Axminster, Charmouth, Bridport, Dorchester and Salisbury. The journey could take 27 hours, quite a bottom-numbing experience for the passengers inside.

Passengers were also often asked to get out and walk alongside the coach. The notorious hills surrounding Charmouth were somewhat of a challenge for the horses pulling the vehicle, so their load was lightened. No one was considered too grand to be told to walk for a while - in 1789 King George III had to get out of the coach while travelling from Weymouth to Sidmouth.

Fortunately for the horses, they didn't have to pull a coach the whole distance - a changeover happened at Winterbourne Abbas on the way to Dorchester and at Honiton en route to Exeter.

One of the most remembered landlords of the coach house was George Holly, who was in charge during the nineteenth century when the inn was frequented by many commercial travellers. One guest, William French, accidently drowned while bathing in 1849 and Holly kindly paid for his funeral. He also held tradesmen's balls - one celebrated the marriage of Victoria, the Princess Royal, in 1858, and another took place to honour the Prince of Wales' marriage in 1863.

Holly left, however, after the fire of 1882. He had disagreed with the owners who chose to pull the building down, so he moved up the hill to Charmouth House. His dislike of the new building was so great that his gravestone in the neighbouring churchyard faces in the opposite direction.

In 1996 the Coach and Horses Hotel was converted into seven flats.

Mediterranea

This photograph, taken in the 1960s, of the top end of The Street opposite the entrance to Higher Sea Lane, shows a shop called Mediterranea, owned by Colonel and Mrs Askwith. The couple often travelled abroad and brought home items to sell that they'd found in Spain, Turkey and other 'exotic' destinations.

The previous owners ran an antique business, but the building has been a grocer's shop and a newsagent's premises selling toys and stationery. In charge was Elizabeth Tarr, a dressmaker, regular churchgoer and a staunch Conservative. So strong were her beliefs that she refused to sell *The Daily Herald*, the paper of the Trade Union Congress in the 1920s. That is, until the news agency threatened to stop all her supplies. After Miss Tarr's death, Portland House, as it's called today, was bought by Charlie How, who converted the house into two flats and added another staircase by cutting off part of the shop. His daughter opened up a hairdressing business. Interestingly, the step of the shop, the top of St Andrew's Church tower parapet and the gate of Stonebarrow farm are all at the same level.

Next door was a bread and cake shop, then the house adjacent is Bayville, which was occupied by William Holly in the late 1870s. Holly was the agent for the London and South Western Railway Company and when he bought the Axminster Bus business, he went to live in a house further down the street named Wistaria.

On the left of this photo, the house with the porch is Badgers Bookshop, which existed until 1968. The porch was added by owner H. Brocklehurst, a retired engineer, who lived there during World War II. Badgers is Grade II listed and estimated to date back to the sixteenth century. It was once an old farm building and dairy, and has also been an establishment selling beer. The local Commissioner of Births and Deaths was a tenant in the 1930s.

Further up you come to Wellhead, an old Jacobean cottage. During the latter part of the nineteenth century, Reuben Durrant lived here and farmed nearby Foxley. Later, a fellow of Magdalen College Oxford, C. R. L. Fletcher, lodged here during the summer holidays. One year he brought a distinguished guest - Cosmo Lang, who was to become Archbishop of Canterbury.

West Beach

The south coast counties of England - Dorset, Hampshire, East Sussex, West Sussex and Kent - enjoy more sunshine than anywhere else in the UK, up to nearly 2,000 hours a year. As Dorset is also less affected by intense Atlantic winds than neighbouring Devon and Cornwall, it can be warmer in winter than the rest of the country by almost nine degrees. Then, because of the configuration of the hills around Charmouth, the area reportedly has lower rainfall in general than nearby Beaminster or Dorchester, meaning it will often miss thunderstorms.

Add to that Charmouth's idyllic beaches, and no wonder the village has been a popular holiday spot for several centuries. Author Jane Austen, a visitor to Lyme Regis in 1803 and 1804, described it as a place of 'high grounds and extensive sweeps of country, and still more, its sweet, retired bay, backed by dark cliffs where fragments of low rock among the sands make it the happiest spot for watching the flow of the tide; for sitting in unwearied contemplation.'

This postcard view of West Beach, taken in the early twentieth century, shows a group of ladies with a small child in the foreground, and boats, beach tents and huts behind. It was in the eighteenth century, when King George III adopted Weymouth as the English Naples, that the 'new craze' of sea bathing took off in Dorset, but at that time, the holiday coast was only really enjoyed by the wealthy and the children of coastguards.

By the mid-nineteenth century, though, everyone was heading to the seaside - Charmouth's Hunter family cashed in and provided bathing machines and swimming lessons. Soon, bathing tents appeared, thereby ending the custom of men going beyond the mouth of the river to bathe while the ladies used bathing machines.

Today, Charmouth has a very distinctive row of blue beach huts at its seafront, famous now for appearing in ITV's *Broadchurch*. The sea at West Beach receives two out of three stars for water quality by the Marine Conservation Society - good news for all the supporters of the annual Christmas Day swim, which sees locals full of festive cheer taking a dip to raise money for the RNLI. An amazing £2,047 was collected in 2014.

Charmouth Post Office

Two buildings seen on The Street today, known as Wistaria and Langley House, were during the first part of the twentieth century the site of Charmouth's village post office, and run for 40 years, first by postmaster William Holly, then his son, also called William.

William senior moved here in the early 1880s to run the Axminster bus service. He had been the agent for the London and South Western Railway Company and had lived at Bayville, further up The Street on the opposite side. Wistaria, however, was large enough to store two buses, and had stables for six horses.

The buses, when full, could seat sixteen passengers - two by the side of the driver, four behind, six people inside, and when the weather would allow, a row of seats for four passengers was bolted on the roof. When that happened, the luggage would be transferred to a wagonette, which would accompany the bus on its journey. A third horse would also be required for a full load, which was ridden by Holly's youngest son, Johnny. He also sometimes stood on the back step and blew the horn.

In 1899 the business was sold to Mrs Pagan of the Coach and Horses and in November 1904 it was passed to Robert Morgan, also of Charmouth. He maintained the route until it ceased in 1911.

Holly set up the post office in 1900. A room at the property was let to the Wilts and Dorset Bank, then when an annex was built, Lloyds Bank took over, opening for two hours a day on a Tuesday and Friday until 1930 when they moved to new premises further down The Street.

The post office relocated to Sunnyside (Devonedge) during World War II. William junior then opened a stationery shop. After his death in 1953, it was to be the County Library for a short while, before an ironmonger's business enlarged the shop. Today you'll find Herringbone, a creative collective whose aim is to support the local community by providing an outlet for artisans and craft makers in the area.

Coronation Procession 1911

This photograph of the village band being followed by locals wearing their finery was taken on 22 June 1911. The procession, to mark the coronation of King George V, was heading down The Street, which had been elaborately decorated for the occasion.

The impressive Victorian house seen in this view, with 'God Bless the Queen' on a banner in front, is Askew House. The property is set back from The Street and literally askew the general building line, which seems to effectively mark the top of the hill and curve of the road. Askew House was built on the site of a small cottage by Richard Oliver of Langport, Somerset, who also bought some of the garden of the neighbouring house so he could alter the front door to face south instead of north. For a long time during the twentieth century, Askew House was the doctor's surgery and residence. Dr Alfred Barratt Hine was residing here at the time of the coronation.

Further up on the right, The Holt was a sweet shop kept by a Lyme man named Burge, then it became a draper's shop and in the 1930s Cecil Gear turned it into a fish shop. Next door, now cottages known as Charm and Heron, was the village Cottage Hospital, established in 1867.

On the bend of the road, where four roads converge and The Street turns into Axminster Road, stood The New Inn, or the New Commercial Inn (there had been another New Inn in the village), built around 1886 after a fire destroyed the thatched property previously standing here. In the early 1900s the pub and hotel were popular with locals and visitors alike, and hunt meetings would regularly congregate here. Every Guy Fawkes Night, up until 1945, tar barrels were lit outside the New Inn then rolled down The Street, guided by men with poles to keep them in the centre of the road. The glorious blaze finished at the Coach and Horses.

The New Inn closed in 1976 and was converted into residential properties.

Albury House and Hillside

This postcard shows Albury House, a charming cottage built in the seventeenth century which once featured on the cover of an AA bed and breakfast guide. TV's famous cookery expert, Fanny Cradock, stayed here as a guest.

The roof has always been thatched, but at one time it was in such a bad condition, it was propped up by a ship's mast. Rev Edmund R. M. White, rector of St Mary's at Catherston Leweston, owned the house in 1891 and his wife, the church organist, erected a memorial stone in the front garden when her beloved dog died. In the mid-1900s, the property became a café with tea garden. Today, it offers self-catering accommodation.

Next are three Regency period detached villas - all Grade II listed, built in 1827. Their gardens, and all those from Omega to The Limes, are bounded on the north side by a stone wall, locally referred to as The Monks' Wall. Back in 1520, the abbots of Forde had invited people to build on parcels of land, each measuring twenty perches by four. As a result, gardens are almost identical in length and width.

In 1849, 3 Hillside was sold to Captain Mould and was occupied by geologist James Harrison. It was later sold to a solicitor, then a surgeon, before Henry Eliot became resident. A talented horseman, Eliot used to break in horses on the beach. He also met 'Buffalo Bill' Cody on a couple of occasions.

The house at 2 Hillside, now a hotel and restaurant called The White House, was owned by Rev Benjamin Jeanes in 1831. At the turn of the twentieth century it was a girls' school, then Sir Cecil Harrison, whose father lived at Little Hurst, moved here. He owned the first motor car in the village, a De Dion Bouton. In 1930 the house became a girls' school again, and in the 1950s it was sold to Prince Charles de Rohan, a descendent of the French noble family.

1 Hillside was first owned by Harriet Prior of Lyme Regis, and the Prior and Templar families lived there until 1953, when it was bought by the Ecclesiastical Commissioners. It then became The Rectory. A lane at the side of the house gave people access to Backlands farm.

The Circus comes to Town

This photo was taken in front of The Arcade, a row of shops built in the 1930s, and captures a time when the circus came to Charmouth. As this image shows, a travelling circus could attract a curious crowd. In 1929, many certainly gathered on the Axminster to Bridport road when a lion escaped its cage while en route to Lyme Regis.

Pasha the lion was part of Chapman's Travelling Menagerie and was being pulled in his cage, which also housed three tigers, by a tractor. However, just west of Charmouth, the tractor experienced some engine trouble and slipped backwards, hitting a tree. With his cage damaged, Pasha - reportedly an exceptional performer and a regular at Blackpool Tower - was able to escape. At first, he seemed quite content on the side of the road. Then the lion tamer turned up, and frightened spectators began to shout, so he bounded a hedge and came upon some cows. A shot was fired, and poor Pasha was killed.

The village in the early 1950s also boasted Noah's Ark Children's Zoo and Tea Gardens, located down Lower Sea Lane. It was open daily from mid-April to October, and admission was sixpence. A village guide at the time claimed that 'amid trees and flowers, you'll find all sorts of unusual animals, housed in most original cages.' Their dwellings had amusing names - Mouse Monastery, Owl Observatory, Hamster Hall and Squirrel Snuggery - and 'the animals are so friendly and really seem to enjoy visitors.' The guide continues to say, 'though this is called a Children's Zoo, the age limit could well be set at 1 to 90 years, so fascinating does it prove to all ages.'

These days, the only animal you are guaranteed to see on Lower Sea Lane is George the giraffe, who stands in the front garden of Hensleigh House Hotel. Okay, so he's stuffed, but according to owners Dawn and Jim Greenfield, George has quite a fan club, receiving a scarf as a Christmas present and a Valentine card from a secret admirer on 14 February.

Old Lyme Road

This stunning view of Charmouth shows Old Lyme Road, the village centre below, and the beautiful countryside at Catherston Leweston, Whitchurch Canonicorum and Conegar Hill beyond. Although one house, Foxley Dene, is clearly seen in the left of this photo, the property doesn't have many neighbours - the fields opposite belonged to Foxley farm and homes you see today on that land, and much of the west cliff, were not built until the 1960s.

It was around this time that Robert Goodden set up a butterfly farm in Old Lyme Road, called Worldwide Butterflies. Robert had been fascinated by butterflies in his parents' garden and surrounding countryside since he was four. Aged twenty, he returned to Charmouth and used part of his family's attic to start his business. Soon it took over the upstairs of their home, then a building was put up in the paddock overlooking the sea and visitors started turning up. In 1966, Goodden and his butterfly collection moved to the grounds of Compton House in Sherbourne.

As it's easily guessed from their names, Old Lyme Road, and the road higher up, Old Lyme Hill, used to be the old route from Charmouth to Lyme Regis. The road became passable in 1826 and went through a deep cutting in the landscape, referred to as the Devil's Bellows (because of the force with which the wind rushed through). It was to be an alternative to the old Roman road which was steep and hazardous. In May 1924, however, after a week of torrential rain and thunderstorms, a landslide closed the coast road. It occurred at the highest point, some 400 feet above sea level, and a newspaper at the time warned people that a 'thousand tons of cliff are gradually moving towards the sea.'

As a result, the road at Fernhill, which had been the old coach road between Bridport and Axminster, came to life again. The bend at the top was widened and the gradient was altered to make it easier for traffic.

Prospect Place

This old photograph was taken around 1870 when George Mortimer was the owner of a grocer's store, located in the same premises as Charmouth Stores today. The shop and three adjacent houses - Ashyford House (now Breeze), Rupert House and Stanley House - are collectively known as Prospect Place, and were built after a fire destroyed the four thatched houses previously standing here. It was on a Saturday evening in June 1864 that flames were seen coming from the roof of one of the houses. Firefighters from Lyme Regis arrived on the scene and removed the thatch covering. As the fire seemed extinguished, they returned home, but by next morning the wind got stronger and a blaze soon started up again, burning the houses to the ground.

It's believed a shop has existed on this spot for 200 years, making it one of the oldest shops in Dorset. At the time of the fire, it was run by John Carter and was also the post office. Prior to that, Samuel Aplin was the man in charge, offering the services of a 'draper, grocer, ironmonger, etc.' He also advertised that he could provide drugs, patent medicines and funerals, and would take orders for new publications, music and music paper, which he would obtain from London.

By the 1880s, E. A. Vince took over and installed a device allowing locals to send telegrams from Charmouth, instead of having to make a trek to Lyme. Apparently you could hear the sound of the needle ticking as you entered the shop. Vince's errand boy, George Ashton, was soon to become the telegraphist before relocating overseas to work in a post office in Ecuador.

A grocer called J. Baker followed, then the Dampiers from Dorchester took over the business. In February 2005, Carol and Phil Tritton became the couple at the helm, along with their son Alex, now married to Maria. Charmouth Stores is today involved with Making a Difference Locally, a charity that helps Nisa stores raise money that can be donated to local charities and good causes. Since joining the scheme, an impressive £1,500 has been raised.

The Court

Buildings have stood on the plot of The Court, the large Regency property with the wooden shutters seen in this old postcard, as far back as the thirteenth century. Almhouses were built here around the 1660s, when a mariner by the name of Anthony Tutchen donated a house and one acre field for the benefit of seamen and their families. Originally he had provided them with shoes and stockings, so imagine their gratitude when they were given a home.

Three cottages situated in the same grounds were made into one large house in 1850 by a Mrs Stuart from Harley Street, London, who also added a drawing room and kitchen. She knocked down the almshouses next door, which were in a bad state of repair, to erect a coach house and stables. The tenants, however, were not made homeless. Instead she purchased a small piece of land in Lower Sea Lane and built two almshouses to accommodate six people. They are now called Hall View.

In time, Mrs Stuart became one of Charmouth's largest landowners. When she died, she owned Stonebarrow farm, the east cliff and several fields in Lower Sea Lane. Her daughter, Catherine, inherited it all aged 54, but on the condition that she must spend at least four months a year living at her family home - and must never marry.

The Schalch family resided at The Court afterwards, and lived here for many years. It became a boarding house in 1932 before being converted into the Court Hotel in 1969, run by Pat and Ken Stapleton. Today, fourteen rooms at The Court are available as office accommodation. In the front grounds, you can still see a circular mound, constructed in the sixteenth or seventeenth century as a viewpoint.

The neighbouring white house on The Street is Monk's Rest, possibly built by the abbots of Forde Abbey. The Stone House, next door, is the only house in the village with a basement kitchen. A naturalist, Mr Sweeting, lived here in the 1840s and when a whale was washed up on Charmouth beach, in his excitement he described it as a new species, Balaenoptera Boops. It was actually a common or fin whale.

Acknowledgments

I would like to thank various people who have kindly supplied pictures and information that have been used in this book. They include Joan Aldworth, Phil Davidson, Richard Dunn, Trish Evans, Sheila and Nick Gilbey, Dawn and Jim Greenfield, Jo and Rob Illingworth, Jill Matthews, Neil Mattingly, Tony Mitcham, Tom Murphy, Helen Parker, Kevin Payne, Andrew Peach, Karen Phillips and Kerry Louise Whatmore.
I would also like to give a special thanks to the Charmouth Local History Society for giving me access to The Pavey Room. *Notes on Charmouth and some of the people who lived there*, written by local historian Reginald W. J. Pavey, has also been an invaluable source.